MARY SCHÄFFER
Adventures in the Canadian Rockies

by MICHALE LANG · Illustrated by KITTY MCLEOD

MARY SCHÄFFER
Adventures in the Canadian Rockies

by MICHALE LANG · Illustrated by KITTY MCLEOD

MARY SCHÄFFER
Adventures in the Canadian Rockies

by MICHALE LANG • Illustrated by KITTY MCLEOD

Mary Schäffer: Adventures in the Canadian Rockies

Published by

Summerthought

Summerthought Publishing
PO Box 2309
Banff, AB T1L 1C1
Canada
www.summerthought.com

1st Edition—2012

Printed in Canada by Friesens.

We gratefully acknowledge the financial support of the Alberta Foundation for the Arts for our publishing activities.

Alberta
Foundation
for the Arts

Library and Archives Canada Cataloguing in Publication

Lang, Michale, 1956- Mary Schäffer adventures in the Canadian Rockies / Michale Lang ; Kitty McLeod, illustrator.
For ages 6-12. ISBN 978-1-926983-07-3
1. Schäffer, Mary T. S. (Mary Townsend Sharples), 1861-1939—Juvenile literature.
2. Women explorers—Rocky Mountains, Canadian (B.C. and Alberta)—Biography—Juvenile literature.
3. Rocky Mountains, Canadian (B.C. and Alta.)—Biography— Juvenile literature. I. McLeod, Kitty, 1958- II. Title.
FC218.S32L36 2012   j971.1'03092   C2012-900415-4

To my family, Dave, Holly and Alec McLeod
with love from Kitty

To my Godchildren, Grace, Sam, and Emma
with love from Auntie Michale

Mary Schäffer loved to explore! When she was a young girl, in the 1860s, her father taught her about nature. They walked for hours in the woods and fields near Chester, Pennsylvania, where they lived. They looked at plants, trees, flowers, and rocks. Mary's family had special beliefs. Her family belonged to a religion called Quaker. When Mary was growing up, most people didn't believe that men and women were equal, but Quakers did.

Although Mary went to excellent schools, she learned much more about science from her explorations in the woods around her home with her father. After school finished each day, Mary took art lessons from Mr. George Lambden. He was a very famous flower painter. Mary enjoyed painting flowers, but she had no idea that flowers would later give her a reason to explore the Canadian Rockies.

When Mary was only four years old, her cousin Jim came to visit. He was different from all of her other relatives. Cousin Jim wore an army uniform, and he had just returned from fighting in the American Indian Wars in the Wild West.

One night, Mary was sent to bed early so that the adults could talk about grown-up matters. But Mary crept out of bed and hid on her own special stool in a corner of the veranda that was covered with vines. Here, she listened to Cousin Jim's thrilling and terrifying tales!

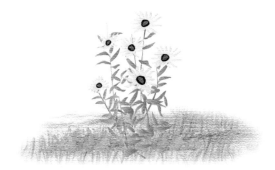

Cousin Jim told a story of how he had come upon the terrible destruction of a First Nations village by other soldiers. Only one baby survived. Cousin Jim had picked up the orphaned babe and taken her to a safe place, but he never knew the poor baby's fate, even after he returned home. Hearing this tragic tale was too much for Mary, and she let out a sob that led to her discovery. She was sent straight to bed, but that sad story stayed with Mary forever.

When Mary was a young woman, she married Dr. Charles Schäffer. They had much in common. He and Mary both loved looking at flowers and exploring nature. On their honeymoon in Toronto, they saw pictures of Lake Louise, and they immediately decided to travel there by train to see the Canadian Rockies. The trip took them more than four days, and they travelled both day and night. After visiting Lake Louise, they continued further west. When they arrived at their hotel, which was called Glacier House, they fell in love with the beautiful mountains, glaciers, and wildflowers.

Charles decided to write a book about the wildflowers of the Canadian Rockies that they saw on their short walks in the area. So they returned each summer, year after year, to find more flowers. Mary said, "Maybe I could help by painting the flowers for your book." Charles liked that idea, so they worked together, observing, gathering, painting, and writing.

But Charles never got to finish his book. He died in 1903, the same year that Mary's mother and father died. Mary was so sad and lonely that she didn't know what to do. All she could think about was how much she missed her loved ones. She thought she might begin to feel better if she could return to her beautiful Canadian Rocky Mountains. So she decided to remember her beloved Charles by finishing his wildflower book. This way, she could go back to her favourite place to do something important.

Mary no longer had enough money to stay at hotels like Glacier House, where she and Charles had stayed together, so she and her friend, Mollie Adams, decided to do something really outrageous. Now remember, during Mary's time, girls were expected to stay home, wear skirts (not pants), and behave themselves. They were not supposed to go off for months at a time into the wilderness and ride horses, sleep in tents, and explore wild areas that hardly anyone else had ever seen.

Mary wrote to Tom Wilson, a guide who took people deep into the mountains on horses. She had met him on one of her trips with Charles. She asked if he could take her to the remote areas she needed to go to discover more wildflowers to finish the book, but he was too busy. He said he could find her another guide. He knew that she had seldom ridden horses and that she hated camping. She had only camped once, at Lake Louise, and she had vowed never to camp again. So Tom had to make sure that the guide he found would be very patient. "Billy Warren is the perfect person for this job. He'll toughen her up," he thought. Billy had come to Canada from England. He had good manners and, like Mary, he loved reading books, but he also knew the ways of the trail. So Billy and his friend, Sid Unwin, became Mary's guides.

But Mary's wilderness training was not without mishaps. One day, as she rode down a mountain on her horse, Eva, Mary noticed that she was sliding towards Eva's ears. Before she could take another breath, she tumbled over her horse's head onto the ground. With her spur still caught in the stirrup, she looked just like a frog! As she glanced back, she saw Eva on her knees with a blanket over her head. Mary could do nothing but laugh uproariously until her guide came to release her.

After one season of training, Mary began to enjoy her wilderness adventures. As soon as she escaped onto the trail where no one except her guides and friends could see her, she crammed her skirt into a pack and put on comfortable pants and a buckskin shirt.

After a few years, she started riding a horse named Mr. Nibs, and he knew exactly who was boss. Mary loved Nibs. To spend four months travelling over unknown wilderness trails in the Canadian Rockies, they needed many horses to carry their camping gear, food, and clothing. And those horses all had minds of their own.

Once when Dandy, one of the packhorses, was crossing a river, he stumbled in the deep, swiftly flowing water and started tumbling over backwards. They had to use their raft to reach him, and as they were rescuing him, all the other horses ran back to the last camp, where they had enjoyed eating the grass and flowers. Mary had to run nearly five kilometres to catch them. Dandy was fine, even though he looked half-drowned after they managed to pull him out.

Some of the most enjoyable times on the trail were around the campfire. After cooking dinner and cleaning up, every night they would share stories about their days and make plans for the next day. Sometimes the mosquitoes were so bad that everyone would have to wear a net to keep them off, and the guides would have to build a really smoky fire so the insects would stay away from the horses.

In the morning, Sid and Billy would pack up the horses and then they would be off for another day of adventure!

Everywhere they went they saw wildlife—bighorn sheep, mountain goats, bears, elk, deer, and moose. Sometimes they would even hear porcupines as the little beasts tried to eat their tent poles or saddles at night after they had gone to bed.

There were not very many people to meet along the trail, but sometimes Mary would encounter Stoney Nakoda people such as Sampson Beaver, his wife Leah, and their daughter, Frances Louise. One summer, Mary remembered to bring a handmade doll for Frances Louise. The little girl loved her doll, and she also loved when Mary took her picture with her family. Mary's Stoney friends could see how much she loved the mountains, so they gave her a special name in their own language: Yahe-weha, meaning "Mountain Woman."

Throughout the summer of 1907, Mary and her friends searched for a lake they had heard about called Chaba Imne, which means "Beaver Lake" in the Stoney Nakoda language. Finally they had to turn back because of snow and cold weather. On the way back, they again met Mary's friend, Sampson Beaver, who drew them a map that helped them find the lake in 1908. The lake became known as Maligne Lake, a famous place today in Jasper National Park.

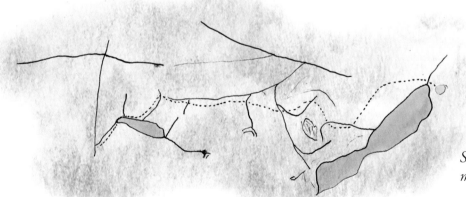

Sampson Beaver's map to Maligne Lake.

In 1911, a few years after Mary and her guides found Chaba Imne, a really amazing thing happened. Even though she wasn't a man, and only men were asked to do such things at the time, Mary was asked by the government to survey Maligne Lake. She would need to measure the position of the lake on the earth, the size of the lake, and the depth so that it could be included on maps of the area. She had never done anything like this before, but she agreed to try.

When Mary went to survey Maligne Lake, she invited her nephew, Paul, who was only 11 years old. Paul had been sick with the whooping cough all winter, but Mary convinced his mother that the fresh air in the mountains would be good for him. Paul was given his own horse, Roany, who was a loyal and gentle friend for the entire trip. One of their guides, Sid Unwin, brought his dog, Mr. Muggins, as the party's mascot.

They needed a boat to do Mary's survey work, so they loaded all the bits and boards it took to build a boat onto Jonas, who was a very strong and patient horse. He carried his awkward load downhill, uphill, across raging rivers, and over Shovel Pass until they reached Maligne Lake. Can you imagine carrying a boat all the way up and over a mountain pass? It's kind of amusing that Shovel Pass got its name because two of the guides who went ahead to dig out the snow for Mary, Jonas and the others, left shovels at the top of the pass to mark the trail.

When they got to Maligne Lake, they immediately set about building their boat, and Mary began her survey. Mr. Muggins did not want to get on the boat at first, but he did not want to be left behind, so eventually, he overcame his fear and jumped aboard.

One of the guides took Paul hunting, and they saw all sorts of wildlife—even a bighorn sheep. Paul also learned how to row the boat and how to fish. Paul loved his time in the mountains.

After many difficult starts and after losing some of her tools at the bottom of the lake, Mary was able to complete her survey. Mary's survey helped make Maligne Lake part of Jasper National Park, which is very important because it has been protected for all the people of Canada to enjoy forever!

All her life, Mary thought that she was a delicate flower, more like a house plant than the wildflowers she painted in the mountains. But her adventures in the Canadian Rockies proved she was as tough as any alpine flower.

The year after Mary completed her survey of Maligne Lake, she moved to Banff because she loved the Canadian Rockies so much. She built a lovely house that she called Tarry-a-while, which is an old-fashioned way of saying "stay a while." As it turned out, she stayed in her favourite place, the beautiful Canadian Rockies until the end of her life. When she wasn't out riding her horse or visiting friends, she spent her time painting, photographing, and writing about her explorations. Her adventurous spirit can still be felt here today.

Image Credits

Illustrations by Kitty McLeod are inspired by Mary Schäffer's lantern slides from the Whyte Museum of the Canadian Rockies. Lantern slides were the first means of showing the same images to a large audience. In the late 19th century, lantern slides were as popular as movies are today. The slides began as black and white photographs that were hand-coloured using special tints. The slide was finished with a mat and glass cover taped to seal the enclosure. They were shown using a projector powered by gas.

Page 23 - *Sampson Beaver Map of Maligne Lake*, 1908, Mary Schäffer fonds (V527/PS 1 – 53), Whyte Museum of the Canadian Rockies